DON'T LOOK
BACK

GETTING UNSTUCK AND MOVING FORWARD
WITH PASSION AND PURPOSE

BIBLE STUDY GUIDE + STREAMING VIDEO
FIVE SESSIONS

CHRISTINE CAINE

Harper*Christian*
Resources

CONTENTS

WELCOME FROM CHRISTINE CAINE!

My husband, Nick, surprised me on my 50th birthday with a Vespa. To enjoy the gift, I had to take a motorcycle safety riding course and pass a written exam.

"Keep your eyes straight ahead," the safety instructor said. "Let your peripheral vision do the work. Remember that where you look, you will go! I don't want to see your head on a swivel. I don't want to see you looking back. Eyes forward!"

Thanks to the instructor's help, I passed the test and earned my license, but one phrase from the instructor resounded in my head: *Where you look, you will go.*

This is not just true when riding a bike, but it's true all throughout our lives. I couldn't help but think …

Where my mind goes, I will go.

Where my emotions go, I will go.

Where my spiritual focus goes, I will go.

But sometimes, like Lot's wife, we're tempted to look back (Genesis 19:26). Now that didn't go well for her, and it rarely goes well for us. What's more, looking back doesn't enable us to go back, and more times than not, it just leaves us stuck. In a place. In a space. In a memory. In a habit. In a mindset. Maybe you're feeling a little stuck in life now.

In the upcoming sessions, we're going to explore the places where it's easy, and all-too-common, to become stuck in life and the tools that we need to start moving forward again into the plans, purposes, and promises of God. I can't wait to make this journey with you.

Chris Caine

HOW TO USE THIS GUIDE

Overview

The *Don't Look Back* Bible study is divided into five sessions. Every session includes Opening Discussion, Video Teaching Notes, Group Discussion Questions, Call to Action, Closing Prayer, and Between Sessions Personal Study. As a group, plan to discuss the opening questions, watch the video, and then use the video notes and questions to engage with the topic. There is complete freedom to decide how best to use these elements to meet the needs of your members. The goal is to develop genuine relationships and become better equipped to share the good news of God's love with others—not just to cover all the material.

Group Size

This five-session video Bible study is designed to be experienced in a group setting such as a Bible study, Sunday school class, retreat, or other small-group or online gathering. If your gathering is large, you may want to consider splitting everyone into smaller groups of five to eight people. This will ensure that there is enough time for everyone to participate in the discussions.

Materials Needed

Everyone in your group will need a copy of this study guide, which includes the opening questions to discuss, notes for the video teachings, directions for activities and discussion questions, and personal studies in between sessions.

You may also get a copy of my *Don't Look Back* book. The videos and materials in this study guide are based on the core biblical principles I teach, as well as my experiences and stories in my book.

Facilitation

Your group will need to appoint a person to serve as a group leader. This person will be responsible for starting the video and keeping track of time during discussions and activities. Group leaders may also read questions aloud and monitor discussions, prompting everyone in the group to respond, and assuring that everyone has the opportunity to participate.

Personal Studies

During the week, you can maximize the impact of this Bible study with the personal study section provided. Treat each personal study section like a devotional and use them in whatever way works best for your schedule. You could do a partial section each day or complete the personal study all in one sitting. These personal studies are not intended to be burdensome or time-consuming, but to help you apply the lessons learned and discussed to your everyday, personal life for growth and connection.

WHERE YOU LOOK, YOU WILL GO

For thirty-plus years now, I've been going to women's conferences, and I don't remember ever hearing a message on Lot's wife, nor do I ever remember teaching one. And yet, of the possible 170 women mentioned in Scripture, she is the only one that Jesus tells us to remember. Why her? Why not Eve, Sarah, Miriam, Deborah, Ruth, Rahab, Esther, Elizabeth, or even Mary, his own mother? Of all the women Jesus could have told us to remember, he mentioned only one, *Lot's wife.*

—Christine Caine, from Chapter 1 of *Don't Look Back*

Opening Discussion

Take five minutes and answer these questions to open your time before jumping into the video session.

1. On a scale of one to ten, check the box that describes how easy is it for you to be part of a study like this.

   1 2 3 4 5 6 7 8 9 10

   It's hard for me to be part of a study like this.   It's easy for me to be part of a study like this.

   _____

   _____

   _____

2. What excites you about being part of this study?

   _____

   _____

   _____

3. What do you hope to get out of this study?

   _____

   _____

   _____

Session One Video (22 minutes)

Group leader, stream the video or play the DVD.

As you watch, take notes on anything that stands out to you.

◆ Vespa story

Look forward, not back

◆ You cannot move forward while you're looking back

◆ Where you look, you will go

◆ Remember Lot's wife

_____

_____

_____

◆ If we look back and linger, we become stuck in the past

_____

_____

_____

_____

◆ Salt is used to preserve

_____

_____

_____

_____

Group Discussion Questions

Group leader, read quotes and commentary aloud and use prompts to guide your discussion time.

I open with a story of taking a motorcycle safety course and the crucial reminder *where you look, you will go*. I write:

> We will always move in the direction of our focus. We'll always end up going to wherever it is that we are looking. Where we look in life is absolutely crucial.

1. What sports or activities have you tried that involve the principle *where you look, you will go*?

   How have you found this principle to be true in your daily life? Spiritual life?

2. Ask a volunteer to read **Hebrews 12:1–2** aloud, and then discuss the following:

   What did Jesus focus on in the most painful part of his journey?

   What are you most focused on right now?

   How pleased are you with the results?

   How would your life be different if your sole focus was Christ?

3. Select a few volunteers to split reading the passages **Genesis 19:15–26** and **Luke 17:28–32**. Discuss the following questions regarding the passages:

What does the angel specifically warn about in Genesis 19:17?

What did Lot's wife desire that caused her to look back longingly and disobey the angel?

Describe a time when you felt torn between what you were leaving and where you were going.

How did you handle the situation?

> "When we work at preserving the past, lingering in nostalgia, we can keep ourselves from the truth of the present and the pain of reality. If we linger in the past, we run the risk of it becoming an idealized version of what really was." —Christine

4. Where do you long for something that once was? That is no more? That can never be again?

Where are you believing that if you linger long enough, you might get back what God told you to leave?

5. Lot's wife disobeyed and became calcified and paralyzed for eternity as a pillar of salt. Circle any of the following where you feel stuck now.

Fears of future	Thoughts	Attitudes	Opinions
Possessions	Hurts	Desires	Disappointments
Comforts	Pains	Wounds	Relationships
Past regrets	Mistakes	Future hopes	Other: _____

Which of these holds you back most? Share your responses with the group.

6. Select a few volunteers to split reading the following passages: **Ephesians 2:8–10**; **Hebrews 6:19**; **Hebrews 13:5**; and **Hebrews 13:8**. Then take some time to meditate on these verses and discuss their significance for you to begin moving forward in faith.

Discuss practical ways you can become unstuck and focus your eyes on Jesus, your author and perfector.

Call to Action

Team up with someone in your group (or online if you are doing this study virtually) and share where you're feeling the most stuck in your life and faith. Tell them a little about your situation and take a moment to pray for each other to find freedom and move forward into all God has for each of you.

Conclusion

Group leader, read aloud to the group to close your time together this week.

It's not always easy to move on when God beckons us forward, especially when things are safe, comfortable, and just the way we like it. Equally, it is often difficult to move on when we have experienced deep trauma, pain, or suffering, and we feel utterly hopeless and helpless. Moving on is something we know we should do, what we often want to do, and at times what we refuse to do, but it remains something God eagerly wants for us.

Wherever you may be on this continuum, may you be able to identify places where you are prone to being stuck, or maybe are stuck, and may you be infused with the strength of the Holy Spirit to take the next step. May you look forward to the future God has for you and keep moving toward it in bold faith—especially when the world is ever-changing.

Closing Prayer

Select a volunteer to read the closing prayer over the group.

Heavenly Father, like Lot's wife, we don't want to look back and linger. We want to move into the fullness of all your plans and desires for us. We know there are areas where we've become stuck and we need you, in your great love, to reveal them. Show us fresh ways to get unstuck and give us the courage to move forward in your purposes and promises. In Jesus' name, amen.

Between Sessions Personal Study

This week's group discussion is just the start, and the goal is to keep digging into where God is calling you to become unstuck and begin moving forward. This section is created as a guide for your personal study time to further explore the topics you discussed with your group. If you're following along with my book, *Don't Look Back*, for the fullest experience of this message, read or review chapters 1–2.

Check in with your group members during the upcoming week and continue the discussion you had with them at your last gathering. Grab coffee, dinner, or reach out by text and share what's going on in your life and heart. Use the following questions to help guide your conversation.

Of all the women in the Bible, Jesus told us to remember Lot's wife (Luke 17:32). The original story in Genesis reveals important details about the culture she lived in and how it may have shaped her.

1. Read **Genesis 19:1–10**. What does this passage reveal about the following?

   Lot and his character:

   _____

   The men of Sodom:

   _____

The angels:

_____

2. Read **Genesis 19:11–13** and **Ezekiel 16:49–50**. What was the great outcry to God against his people?

_____

_____

How did those in Sodom and Gomorrah neglect God and his priorities?

_____

_____

_____

Which of these priorities are you tempted to neglect?

_____

_____

_____

3. Read **Genesis 19:14–17**. When Lot hesitated, how was he shown the mercy of God?

_____

_____

_____

What specific instructions does the angel give the family? (Hint: v. 17)

_____

_____

_____

4. Read **Genesis 19:18–26**. Placing yourself in Lot's wife's shoes, which of the following do you think prompted her to disobey the messengers of God and look back longingly? Place a star next to any that might apply.

The life she knew   Her home   Extended family and friends

Familiarity   Nostalgia   Prominence in the community

Like most everyone, when the pandemic of 2020 spilled over into 2021, I was tempted to look back. To want to go back to 2019—or any year of our lives before 2020. To go back to normal, whatever our normal was. To forget the new normal that we were all desperately trying to create. Yet, no matter how much I longed to go back to normal, there was no going back. That world as we knew it was finished and God was beckoning me, along with everyone else, to move forward, to lay hold of his purpose and promises in the future.

Sorting through the tension of not looking back and trying to move forward—including trying to figure out how to move at all in a locked-down world—I began reminding myself that while the world had changed, God had not. He was the same as he'd always been, and I could depend on him to guide me forward.

5. We all have places where we find ourselves stuck looking back longingly. Take a few moments to ask God to show you places where you have been (or are) stuck looking back longingly. List them here.

◆ _____

◆ _____

◆ _____

◆ _____

◆ _____

6. As you look over the list of what you are longing for, ask God to show you the deeper issue that may be behind each one. For example, if you're longing to move back to a place you once lived, the deeper desire may be to know and be known through relationships. Or if you're longing for a particular role (i.e., wife, mother, manager, etc.), the deeper desire may be for significance. Write your reflections below.

◆ _____

_____

_____

◆ _____

_____

_____

7. Now, reflect on what God's Word says and how he wants to meet you in those longings. Does God want to meet you with his comfort as you long for what was and is lost? Does God want you to look to him as the true source of fulfillment for that longing? Does God want to refine that longing? Write down verses that God leads you to for each question. Here are a few to get you started: **Joshua 1:9**; **John 16:33**; **Romans 12:2**; **Romans 15:13**; and **Philippians 2:3–4**.

   ◆

   ◆

   ◆

   ◆

8. Read **Luke 17:32–33**. According to Jesus, what's the key to preserving life?

What happens to those who try to keep their life?

_____

_____

_____

Losing your life to God means looking to God to find out what he wants you to do, and then doing it. One of the most powerful things we can do is take an internal, spiritual inventory so we don't get stuck doing the things we've always done, the way we've always done them, or coasting on our past accomplishments.

Take some time to do your own personal inventory. Begin by asking the Holy Spirit, "What is on your heart that you want to do in and through my life?" Then take a few moments to write down anything that comes to mind.

_____

_____

_____

_____

_____

_____

_____

_____

9. Continue this time in prayer by answering the questions in the chart below.

PRAYERFUL QUESTIONS	RESPONSE
What do you want to do and shape in my life personally?	
What do you want to do and shape in my professional life?	
What do you want to do and shape in my family?	
What do you want to do and shape in my friends?	
What do you want to do and shape in my church community?	
Who do you want to reach with the love and message of Christ through me?	
How are you calling me to participate in this world?	

As you review your responses, consider if there is something that you need to challenge or something you need to risk, including failure. Next, consider if God has already placed a seedling of something new that he wants to grow in you as you move onward, upward, and forward.

Where do you know of . . .

a wrong that you want to make right?

_____

_____

_____

a suffering that you want to end?

_____

_____

_____

a hurt that you want to heal?

_____

_____

_____

a loss that you want to restore?

_____

_____

_____

> We all have places where we're tempted to look back longingly, but we don't have to get stuck there.

In chapter 2 of *Don't Look Back*, "Prepare Your Heart to Go," I write the following reminder:

> In all the transitions I've lived through, I've learned that just because something has died, God's promises, plans, and purposes for my life have not. In fact, they are still very much alive. I know there are times when life upends us and we have to accept what we don't want to accept, but I have found that if we can separate the circumstances we're facing from God's overall purpose for our lives, then we can have the hope we need to keep moving forward.

Write a prayer on the lines below asking God to help you gain traction in the places where you've become stuck.

_____

_____

_____

_____

_____

_____

_____

_____

_____

_____

_____

_____

_____

_____

KNOWING WE ARE CHILDREN OF THE KING

Knowing that I have been adopted into God's family, that I am his child, is the source of my confidence. There is nothing more intimate God could have done than to adopt us, and when we are confident that he sees us, knows us, and loves us, we can live our lives unafraid. We can step out in faith and step into the unknown future fully confident that our God is with us, for us, protecting us, and guiding us. We can face the inevitable ups and downs of life with assurance that God is our heavenly Father, and he is willing to help us.

—**Christine Caine**, from Chapter 3 of *Don't Look Back*

Opening Discussion

Take five minutes and answer these questions to open your time before jumping into the video session.

1. What experiences have you had with adoption—whether personal or through a friend—that most shaped your understanding of adoption?

2. What does it mean to you to be adopted by God?

Session Two Video (23 minutes)

Group leader, stream the video or play the DVD.

As you watch, take notes on anything that stands out to you.

◆ Awakening at doctor's office

_____

_____

_____

_____

◆ Adopted into God's family

_____

_____

_____

_____

◆ As God's children, we have rights, privileges, and blessings

_____

_____

_____

_____

◆ No longer a slave but a son and heir

_____

_____

_____

_____

◆ Adoption was God's Plan A

_____

_____

_____

_____

◆ God loves you perfectly, wholly, completely

_____

_____

_____

_____

Group Discussion Questions

Group leader, read quotes and commentary aloud and use prompts to guide your discussion time.

> "I begin with a story of realizing I didn't know my biological family's medical history because I'd been adopted. I said, 'Knowing I'd been adopted by God gave me a sense, a deep sense of identity and stability, when everything in my world was spiraling. It gave me a sense of belonging, security, and significance. When we don't know who we are and whose we are, we can easily believe all kinds of things about ourselves that are not from God, and get stuck trying to gain our identity from other things.'" —Christine

1. Where are you tempted to find your identity other than Christ? (Ex. accomplishments, titles, possessions, experiences)

   In what did you once find your identity?

   What helped set you free from finding your identity in that?

2. Select a few volunteers to split reading the passage **Galatians 4:1–7** aloud and then discuss the following:

What does it mean to you personally to be a child of God?

In what ways are you still behaving or acting like a servant rather than an heir?

What is holding you back from entering the full privileges of being an heir of God?

3. Ask a volunteer to read **Ephesians 1:4–6**. Discuss the following questions regarding the passages:

What is the foundation for adoption as a child of God?

What are you destined for according to this passage?

> "God is not a cold, distant, aloof, angry, or tyrannical father. He is a loving, kind, gracious, and compassionate father. His love for us is perfect and complete. He knows everything about us, even the stuff deep in our hearts that nobody else knows. And you know what? He still chose us to be his daughter or his son, and his heir. You are fully seen. You are fully known. And you are fully loved. There is nothing you can do to make God love you any more or any less." —Christine

4. Share these prompts with the group:

What encourages you the most in this statement?

What challenges you the most in this this statement?

What in your past hinders you from seeing God as the perfect, loving Father?

5. Discuss some of the following questions:

Where have you become stuck in shame, guilt, condemnation, fear, or death?

Where have you become stuck in the negativity someone has spoken over your life?

6. Discuss practical ways you can become unstuck and live as a beloved child and heir of God.

Call to Action

Team up with someone in your group (or online if you are doing this study virtually) and share where you long to live in the fullness of being a child of God. Tell them a little about your situation and take a moment to pray for each other, to find your identity and security, and move forward into all God has for each of you.

Conclusion

Group leader, read aloud to the group to close your time together this week.

The family of God is for whosoever will come. Because of Jesus' life, death, and resurrection, God takes us into his family and establishes us as his children. Adoption is at the heart of the Gospel. God could have used any metaphor to explain how he saved us or how we became part of his family. But he used this intimate metaphor of adoption to show us that he willingly chose us to be his children because he loves us.

You don't have to get stuck in shame, guilt, condemnation, or fear. You don't have to get stuck in the negativity that anyone has ever spoken over your life. You don't have to get stuck in any of these places. You don't have to look back. You can keep moving forward in the knowledge that you are a beloved child of God.

Closing Prayer

Select a volunteer to read the closing prayer over the group.

Heavenly Father, thank you for adopting us as your children through Jesus' death and resurrection. Help us identify any areas in which we are placing our value or trust other than you. Show us where we've become entangled and stuck. In your love, reveal them and set us free. We want you to be the sole source of our identity and security so we can move into the fullness of your plans and purposes as beloved children of God. In Jesus' name, amen.

Between Sessions Personal Study

This week's group discussion is just the start, and the goal is to keep digging into where God is calling you to live as his beloved child. This section is created as a guide for your personal study time to further explore the topics you discussed with your group. If you're following along with my book, *Don't Look Back*, for the fullest experience of this message, read or review chapters 3–4.

Check in with your group members during the upcoming week and continue the discussion you had with them at your last gathering. Grab coffee, dinner, or reach out by text, and share what's going on in your life and heart. Use the following questions to help guide your conversation.

It's hard to believe now, but in 1966, I was literally considered to be an illegitimate child. It was based on a belief that developed in the nineteenth century that children born out of wedlock were a public health threat. They were labeled illegitimate, considered outcasts, and seen as inferior to members of legitimate families led by married couples. They were often publicly shamed and received community disapproval.

Can you imagine? How could anyone label a baby an outcast? Or socially inferior? All because of their parents' marital status? It's unconscionable, and yet, it has gone on throughout history all around the world. But to be honest, I've learned that the feeling of being illegitimate can happen to any of us.

1. Where have you experienced feelings of being illegitimate?

_____

_____

_____

2. How do you cope or deal with those feelings?

_____

_____

_____

The feelings of illegitimacy can rise when we feel out of place, as though we don't belong. When we feel unwelcome, sized up, or less than. When we feel dismissed, marginalized, or insecure. When we're flat-out rejected or cancelled. When we feel we have to perform to be accepted, but we can never perform enough. If you've ever been labeled illegitimate—and I would guess all of us have, explicitly or implicitly—then you know how painful a label it is, and you know how powerful it is. You know how it robs you of freedom, as it binds you in strongholds of fear, shame, and guilt.

Take some time to reflect on the presence of shame, fear, and guilt in your life. Try to assess if they are weights that you are carrying currently (and to what degree), rather than how you've experienced them historically.

3. Fill out the table below with the following: the heaviness of the weight (1 = little; 10 = great) and the specifics of the weight.

◆ What do you feel shame about?

◆ What are you fearful of?

◆ What do you feel guilt over?

WEIGHT	HEAVINESS OF WEIGHT (1–10)	SPECIFICS OF THE WEIGHT
Shame		
Fear		
Guilt		

The presence of shame, fear, and guilt can signal that we have taken on the label of "illegitimate" in some area of our lives, and often, we pick up that label through our experiences, including things that have been said or done to us.

4. Think through the following types of experiences, reflecting on:

◆ What was said or done

◆ The message I received from it

TYPE OF EXPERIENCE	WHAT WAS SAID OR DONE	MESSAGE I RECEIVED
Words spoken to me		
Words spoken about me		
Rejection (social, professional, etc.)		

TYPE OF EXPERIENCE	WHAT WAS SAID OR DONE	MESSAGE I RECEIVED
Abandonment		
Mistakes		
Other		

It's crucial that we know who we are in Christ, that we know we have been adopted into the kingdom of God, that we are sons and daughters and heirs.

This is where our legitimacy lies. We are meant to live securely in the love of God, knowing we are neither illegitimate nor orphans, but his beloved children. However, we often outsource the source of our security by making others our authority, and by placing their opinions of us above God's truth about us.

If we do this long enough, then it can lead us off course from God's purposes and onto a personal quest to seek our value, worth, and belonging from those who can't give it to us—be it our spouses, our children, our friends, our mentors, our colleagues, our bosses, or our followers.

5. Our interactions and experiences do not define who we are. God does. Look up the verses below and fill in who they say we are in Christ.

VERSE	WHO I AM IN CHRIST
John 15:15	
Romans 5:1	
Romans 8:1–2	
1 Corinthians 6:17	

VERSE	WHO I AM IN CHRIST
1 Corinthians 6:19–20	
Ephesians 2:6	
Ephesians 2:10	
Philippians 3:20	
Colossians 1:13–14	

6. As you reflect on who you are in Christ, go back to what you wrote in the first table regarding the weight you're carrying and the heaviness of that weight. How specifically does knowing who you are in Christ free you from . . .

◆ what you feel shame about:

_____

_____

_____

◆ what you are fearful of:

_____

_____

_____

◆ what you feel guilty about:

_____

_____

_____

> The next time the enemy tries to label you as illegitimate—unloved and unwanted—don't accept the label. God has adopted you into his family, made you his daughter or son, and wants you to live secure in his everlasting, never-ending love.

In chapter 3 of *Don't Look Back*, "Go Knowing We Are Who He Says We Are," I write the following reminder:

> Knowing we are his sons and daughters, his beloved, is what God wants us to be convinced of, because knowing how very much we are loved and wanted is what helps us keep moving forward when everything and everyone is telling us otherwise.

Write a prayer on the lines below asking God to help you realize and experience the depths of his unending love to move you forward in life.

_____

_____

_____

_____

_____

_____

_____

_____

_____

_____

_____

_____

GOING AGAIN FOR THE PROMISES OF GOD

"There's nothing that will challenge your faith more than going again and seeing nothing, especially when it has to do with a promise from God that has gone unfulfilled for weeks or months or years. But even then, in my life and yours, we have to risk going again."

—Christine Caine, from Chapter 5 of *Don't Look Back*

Opening Discussion

Take five minutes and answer these questions to open your time before jumping into the video session.

1. Which of the following best describes your current prayer life? Explain why you chose that description.

   Quiet   Vibrant   Stuck   Rich   Natural

   Disappointing   Frustrating   Hard   Fabulous   Nonexistent

   _____

   _____

   _____

   _____

2. If you could change one thing about your prayer life, what would it be?

   _____

   _____

   _____

   _____

Session Three Video (23 minutes)

Group leader, stream the video or play the DVD.

As you watch, take notes on anything that stands out to you.

◆ Story of girls rescued from Uzbekistan

◆ God still does miracles in the twenty-first century

◆ Prayer precedes miracles

◆ A little cloud like a man's hand

◆ Nothing will test your faith like nothing

◆ Our shoulders are not broad enough to carry the burdens of this world

Group Discussion Questions

Group leader, read quotes and commentary aloud and use prompts to guide your discussion time.

> "In my book, I share the miraculous story of eleven girls being rescued from Uzbekistan in response to prayer." —Christine

1. Describe a time when God answered prayer in a way that astounded you.

   How did this change the way you knew and experienced God and his character?

2. Select a few volunteers to split reading the passages **Psalm 77:14**; **1 John 5:14**; and **Mark 11:24**. Respond to the following prompts regarding the passages:

   What do these passages reveal about prayer?

   Describe how you've experienced these truths in your life.

"Not everything we pray for gets answered in the way that we hope or imagine. But God listens to us and hears every word. Sometimes we must persist in prayer and not give up just because it looks like nothing is happening. The risk of going again and praying again is so worth it. God is always moving, and God is always acting—even if we can't see it."
—Christine

3. On a scale of one to ten, how challenging is it for you to persist in prayer? When are you most tempted to give up praying for something or someone?

   What's one long-time prayer you still ache for God to answer in the way you want?

4. Select a few volunteers to split reading **1 Kings 18:41–46** and **James 5:17–18**, and then discuss the following:

   Why do you think Elijah persisted in prayer even after the servant saw nothing six times?

   How would you have responded if you were the servant?

   Describe a time in the past or present when you sensed God was up to something, even when nothing testified to that fact.

"It takes courage to go back because when we go again, there's the risk that we're not going to see anything. We risk being disappointed, discouraged, and disillusioned. But when you go again, there's also a reward. God's Word is full of life and hope. To see the promises of God activated in our lives, we have to pray, believe, and speak what he says. We must risk praying again and again and again with expectation, if that's what it takes to see the promises of God come to pass in our lives." —Christine

5. Where have you become stuck in discouragement or disillusionment in your prayer life?

   How does that hinder the way you pray today?

   How does Elijah's story encourage you to pray with faith and expectation again?

6. Discuss the following:

   What empowers you to continue believing in faith and praying when you can't see anything happening?

   Where do you most need to double down in prayer until you experience breakthrough?

Discuss practical ways you can become unstuck in prayer and experience the renewal and recharging that happens when you take all your concerns to Jesus.

Call to Action

Team up with someone in your group (or online if you are doing this study virtually) and share where you're feeling the most stuck in prayer. Tell them a little about your situation and where you need to see God move in a powerful way. Take time to pray for each other over the upcoming week—and then continue to pray persistently in faith throughout this study.

Conclusion

Group leader, read aloud to the group to close your time together this week.

In this age that's full of fear, chaos, suffering, injustice, and division, we must get good at praying again. We won't make it without prayer. Let's learn to give our concerns to God and to cast our cares on him because he cares for us.

Prayer is an act of spiritual renewal. It restores us; it recharges us; it reinvigorates us. It sets our eyes on the only one who can do something to change our circumstances. You and I can't change people, but God can do anything. In Jesus, there's always a cloud of hope. It's time to rise up and go to God as many times as it takes, until we experience breakthrough.

Closing Prayer

Select a volunteer to read the closing prayer over the group.

Heavenly Father, increase our faith and renew our hope. Heal any areas of disappointment and disillusionment. By your Spirit, align our desires with your desires. Multiply our readiness and longing to pray. Help us to persist, even when we don't see the results that we want on the timeline we desire. Give us the courage to go again with holy expectation that you will work in miraculous and mighty ways for our good and your glory. In Jesus' name, amen.

Between Sessions Personal Study

This week's group discussion is just the start to reigniting your prayer life, and the goal is to keep digging into where God is working specifically in you. This section is created as a guide for your personal study time to further explore the topics you discussed with your group. If you're following along with my book, *Don't Look Back,* for the fullest experience of this message, read or review chapter 5.

Check in with your group members during the upcoming week and continue the discussion you had with them at your last gathering. Grab coffee, dinner, or reach out by text, and share what's going on in your life and heart. Use the following questions to help guide your conversation.

For Elijah, the length of time it took to feel rain was the length of time it took for his servant to run back and forth seven times. While Elijah's servant was physically going again, Elijah was spiritually going again, going back to what God said.

I don't know what went through the servant's mind that whole time, but I know from experience there's nothing that will challenge your faith like *nothing*, especially when it has to do with a promise from God that you have been praying for over the course of weeks, months, or years. But even then, in my life and yours, we have to risk going again. We have to risk praying in faith, believing, and proclaiming the promises of God before we see them.

1. What do each of the following passages reveal about the role of persistence in prayer?

   Luke 18:1:

   _____

   _____

   Luke 22:42–44:

   _____

   _____

   Romans 12:12:

   _____

   _____

   Ephesians 6:18:

   _____

   _____

   James 5:1–9:

   _____

   _____

2. The Bible contains many examples of "going again" in Scripture. Look up the following passages and note the motivation(s) to go again.

   In **Exodus 33:12–23**, Moses goes again in intercession. What motivated him to go again?

   _____

   _____

   In Esther 5 and 7, Esther makes repeated requests of the king. Look at **Esther 4:12–16**. What motivated her to go again?

   _____

   _____

3. Over and over in the Scriptures we see Paul go again. What do the following verses reveal about what motivated him?

   Acts 20:24:

   _____

   _____

   Galatians 2:20:

   _____

   _____

   Philippians 3:7–14:

   _____

   _____

4. Despite being hated, mistreated, and rejected by so many, Jesus spent his life and ministry declaring and demonstrating that the kingdom of God was at hand. What motivated him to go again and again according to the following passages?

John 5:17:

John 5:19:

John 12:49:

5. All throughout history, God has gone again and again, persevering in pursuit of and patience with people despite thousands of years of being rejected by them. What, among other things, leads God to go again according to the following passages?

John 3:16:

2 Peter 3:9:

_____

_____

6. In what area(s) of your life do you sense God is calling you to go again?

_____

_____

_____

_____

What specifically has he said in his Word or by his Spirit in prayer to let you know that he is calling you to go again?

_____

_____

_____

What specific action steps do you need to take over the following time frame to be faithful to go again in this area?

Today:

_____

_____

_____

This week:

_____

_____

_____

This month:

_____

_____

_____

This year:

_____

_____

_____

_____

_____

Going again can affect almost every area of our lives. In this session, we applied it primarily to prayer—and going again in prayer when we've been disappointed with the results.

Reflect on anything you've prayed about but perhaps have backed away from because you haven't seen the answer you had hoped. How did this make you feel? And what did this make you think about God that may be untrue?

7. Fill in the chart below.

WHAT HAVE YOU PRAYED FOR BUT HAVEN'T SEEN THE RESULT YOU HOPED?	WHAT EMOTION DID YOU FEEL FROM THE LACK OF RESULTS?	WHAT DID THIS MAKE YOU THINK ABOUT GOD THAT MAY BE UNTRUE?

WHAT HAVE YOU PRAYED FOR BUT HAVEN'T SEEN THE RESULT YOU HOPED?	WHAT EMOTION DID YOU FEEL FROM THE LACK OF RESULTS?	WHAT DID THIS MAKE YOU THINK ABOUT GOD THAT MAY BE UNTRUE?

WHAT HAVE YOU PRAYED FOR BUT HAVEN'T SEEN THE RESULT YOU HOPED?	WHAT EMOTION DID YOU FEEL FROM THE LACK OF RESULTS?	WHAT DID THIS MAKE YOU THINK ABOUT GOD THAT MAY BE UNTRUE?

When it comes to prayer, one of the most powerful actions we can take is to use God's Word to shape our prayers. Psalm 119:105 describes God's Word as a lamp for our feet and a light to our path. Like Elijah, we often find ourselves caught between the sound of rain and when the rain actually comes. That's when we have to walk by faith and not by sight, choose to continue to trust God even when we can't trace him, and stand on God's Word and the truth of what God reveals about himself.

8. Reflecting on the previous chart, what are the verses you've been standing on in prayer regarding your requests? If you have them, write them in the chart below. If not, go to God's Word and search for God's promises regarding what you're asking him to do. Personalize such verses and pray God's Word back to him in the chart below. Here are a few suggested verses: **Joshua 1:9**; **Psalm 84:11**; **Psalm 100:5**; **Isaiah 43:2**; **Jeremiah 24:7**; **Matthew 6:31–33**; **Matthew 11:28–30**; and **2 Corinthians 9:8**.

WHAT YOU'VE PRAYED FOR BUT HAVEN'T SEEN THE RESULT YOU HOPED:	BIBLE PROMISE YOU'LL STAND ON REGARDING YOUR PRAYER REQUEST:	SCRIPTURE-BASED PRAYER FOR WHAT YOU'RE ASKING GOD TO DO:

WHAT YOU'VE PRAYED FOR BUT HAVEN'T SEEN THE RESULT YOU HOPED:	BIBLE PROMISE YOU'LL STAND ON REGARDING YOUR PRAYER REQUEST:	SCRIPTURE-BASED PRAYER FOR WHAT YOU'RE ASKING GOD TO DO:

9. List three times you prayed in faith with expectation and saw God respond in power.

1. _____

_____

_____

2. _____

_____

_____

3. _____

_____

How does reflecting on God's power and faithfulness in the past empower you to pray with faith and expectation for the future?

> If we are going to grasp the promises of God, then we've got to get good at going again. We can't stop going just because we don't see a cloud the first time or the second time or the third or the fourth or the fifth or the sixth. We must become tenacious Christians who keep going as many times as it takes in faith-filled prayer.

In chapter 5 of *Don't Look Back*, "Take the Risk and Go Again," I write the following reminder:

> When Elijah prayed for rain, it was God's promise to send rain that served as the basis for Elijah's persistence. He had one word from God, and he stepped out in bold faith proclaiming that it would rain before there was any natural reason to proclaim rain . . . What was the source of Elijah's confidence? It wasn't that Elijah wanted it. It wasn't that Elijah said it. It was that God, who keeps his Word, had said it. It's powerful when we move forward in faith, especially when we can't see anything to confirm our prayers—but that's exactly what faith does.

Write a prayer on the lines below asking God to help you grow your faith and expectation for him to move in unexpected and powerful ways.

_____

_____

_____

_____

_____

_____

_____

_____

_____

_____

_____

_____

_____

_____

A LITTLE CAN DO A LOT

A sense of entitlement can be subtle, tucked away in our hearts, causing us to think we deserve more than we have, and that God could not possibly want us to do more if he is not going to give us more to do more with. The fact is that God tends to work the opposite way; he wants us to give him all of whatever it is that we have, so that he can do so much more than we could ever ask or hope with our little. If we keep waiting to have more to do more, we will stay stuck.

—Christine Caine, from Chapter 6 of *Don't Look Back*

Opening Discussion

Take five minutes and answer these questions to open your time before jumping into the video session.

1. On a scale of one to ten, check the box that describes how much you wrestle with procrastination. Then discuss what contributes to your procrastination.

   1   **2**   **3**   **4**   **5**   **6**   **7**   **8**   **9**   **10**

   I don't procrastinate   I tend to procrastinate
   at all.   all the time.

2. When God calls you to something new, do you tend to see it as an invitation or an interruption? Explain.

_____

_____

_____

_____

_____

_____

_____

Session Four Video (19 minutes)

Group leader, stream the video or play the DVD.

As you watch, take notes on anything that stands out to you.

◆ Story of first ministry positions and A21

_____

_____

_____

_____

◆ Widow of Zarephath

_____

_____

_____

_____

◆ The unlikely places that God sends us

_____

_____

_____

_____

◆ She had the ingredients for a miracle, but couldn't see it

_____

_____

_____

_____

_____

◆ Obedience gets us unstuck

_____

_____

_____

_____

_____

◆ What we think limits us doesn't limit God

_____

_____

_____

_____

_____

Group Discussion Questions

Group leader, read quotes and commentary aloud and use prompts to guide your discussion time.

> "God has always tended to use highly unlikely people in highly unlikely places to do highly unlikely things that bring him great glory. Now, this means that if you don't feel qualified, if you don't feel worthy or capable or educated enough or talented enough for God to use you for His purposes here on Earth, then you're likely to be the most likely person that God wants to use." —Christine

1. When it comes to starting something new, discuss which of the following you tend to wrestle with most: Feeling unqualified. Feeling unworthy. Feeling incapable. Feeling uneducated. Feeling untalented.

   What in your life caused you to feel or think that way?

   What has God been calling, leading, nudging you toward, but you've hesitated to do because you feel self-doubt?

2. On the continuum below, mark when you tend to think God wants to use you in a significant way?

God wants to use me
right where I am,
here today.

God wants to use me
sometime, somewhere
in the future.

How do you suspect God wants to use you right where you are now in this season of life?

3. Select a few volunteers to split reading the passage **1 Kings 17:10–16** aloud, and then discuss the following:

What ingredients did the widow have for a miracle?

What did Elijah say to the widow to encourage her faith?

What role did obedience play in the woman experiencing the miracle?

"Often you and I are just like that woman. God asks us to give something, to do something, and we answer, 'I don't have it. I can't. I'm not enough. I'm not gifted enough. I'm not talented enough. I don't have enough.' What we focus on first and foremost is what we don't have, instead of looking at what we do have now." —Christine

4. Discuss on which you tend to focus: what you have or what you don't have.

   How does each way of believing affect your relationships, work, or spiritual life?

5. Discuss the following:

   What gifts, talents, and resources do you have in your unlikely place?

   How have you been devaluing what you've been given and entrusted with?

   What little has God given you that He wants to make much with?

"God has always used our little to do a lot. Moses had a little rod. With it, God parted the Red Sea. David had a little slingshot and some stones. With them, God took down Goliath. A boy had some bread and fish. With them, God fed over twenty thousand people. In each, God worked through something small to do something big. God gave each person an invitation and a choice to participate in the purposes of God exactly in the place where he placed him." —Christine

6. Where in your life are you playing it safe or thinking too small?

Where is the fear of failing holding you back from God's plans and purposes for your life?

What's the small next step God is calling you to take to get unstuck from where you are so that he can take you to where you're going?

Call to Action

Team up with someone in your group (or online if you are doing this study virtually) and share where you're feeling God is leading you to step out in faith and obedience. Tell them a little about your situation, and take a moment to pray for each other to have courage to obey and watch God do a lot with a little.

Conclusion

Group leader, read aloud to the group to close your time together this week.

When we put our little in the hands of a big God, things happen. Not any one of us has the ability or the capacity to do all that God has called us to do on our own. But when we give him a little, when we invite him to do what only he can do, he helps us to move forward into all the plans and the purposes that he has for our lives.

Closing Prayer

Select a volunteer to read the closing prayer over the group.

Heavenly Father, we want to be people who offer all we have to you. We want to be vessels of your love, grace, and truth, and to encourage those who fulfill your purposes in our generation. Help us to be quick to perceive what you are doing, ready to accept your call as an invitation, willing to offer up whatever you've placed in our hands, and faithful to run the race you've assigned to us. We know through you, a little can do a whole lot. In Jesus' name, amen.

Between Sessions Personal Study

This week's group discussion is just the start, and the goal is to keep digging into where God is calling you. This section is created as a guide for your personal study time to further explore the topics you discussed with your group. If you're following along with my book, *Don't Look Back*, for the fullest experience of this message, read or review chapters 6–7.

Check in with your group members during the upcoming week, and continue the discussion you had with them at your last gathering. Grab coffee, dinner, or reach out by text, and share what's going on in your life and heart. Use the following questions to help guide your conversation.

Too often, we're tempted to minimize what we've been given—especially when it appears little—rather than value it as God does.

1. Read **Zechariah 4:10**. Why do we tend to "despise" the little?

What leads you to look down on the little?

Sometimes, I think we despise it because of its costs. When something is just starting, whether a project, a business, or our education, for example, everything about it is hard. Everything. And we can be tempted to "despise" it because of what it will require from us—investment, time, energy, sacrifice, and so much more.

If we are not careful, we can come to believe that the cost of our action will be greater than the cost of our inaction, and that the cost of our obedience will be greater than the cost of our disobedience—which it never is.

2. When we find ourselves despising what seems small on account of its anticipated cost, we need to remind ourselves and our souls whom we serve. Look up the following passages. What does each one reveal about the character or nature of God?

   Psalm 103:8:

   _____

   Isaiah 40:28:

   _____

   Isaiah 40:29:

   _____

   Philippians 4:19:

   _____

3. Circle the passage on the previous page that you think will be most crucial for you to remember when you're being led to step out in faith and start something new. Why is that particular passage so meaningful?

4. Another reason we may despise the little is because of fear, including fear of failure. On the continuum below, mark how much you wrestle with fear of failure.

1　**2**　**3**　**4**　**5**　**6**　**7**　**8**　**9**　**10**

I don't wrestle　　　　　　　　　　　I'm overcome
with fear of failure.　　　　　　　with fear of failure.

What do the following passages reveal about our fight with fear and self-doubt?

Deuteronomy 31:6:

Psalm 27:1:

Psalm 46:1–3:

_____

_____

2 Timothy 1:7:

_____

_____

A third reason we can despise our "little" is due to our feelings of entitlement:

◆ If God wanted me to do more, he would have given me more.

◆ God wouldn't want me to be uncomfortable.

◆ God just wants to bless me.

◆ God just wants me to be happy.

5. Reflecting on the list above, underline the one you tend to wrestle with most. How can entitlement hold you back from moving forward in faith?

_____

_____

_____

_____

_____

_____

_____

A fourth factor in despising the little is ambition, which can lead us to despise small beginnings. When we don't want to do what God is calling us to do—because in our eyes it doesn't appear successful, glamourous, significant, influential, appealing, valued, large, or important enough—we can be sure this is at work. We need to repent of our selfish ambition and replace it with godly ambition, which will cause us to see opportunities to have kingdom impact in what can appear to be insignificant opportunities.

6. What's one thing you've sensed God nudging or leading you to do, but you resisted because it felt insignificant or beneath you? Write a prayer of repentance in the space below.

7. Prayerfully reflect on times God has called you to step out and do something that seemed small and insignificant. Which of the following impacted you? How did it impact you?

Cost:

_____

_____

_____

Fear:

_____

_____

Entitlement:

_____

_____

Ambition:

_____

_____

_____

Other:

_____

_____

_____

As you contemplate your answers to the previous questions, what do you want your responses to be the next time that God calls you to step out and get started, even when you have a little or what he calls you to do seems small?

_____

_____

_____

_____

What practices and commitments can you put in place to respond that way?

_____

_____

_____

_____

Many of us tend to see limitation more than we recognize provision, but God has blessed us with many kinds of resources: our experiences, relationships, work, abilities, talents, gifts, education, possessions, finances, and so much more.

8. Take some time to identify resources that God has given you and list how you are using those for his purposes. Also, pray and ask if there are any next steps God wants you to take to use those resources for his purposes.

TYPE	SPECIFIC RESOURCE	HOW YOU ARE USING IT FOR HIS PURPOSES	STEPS TO USE THIS RESOURCE FOR HIS PURPOSES MORE
Experiences			
Relationships			

TYPE	SPECIFIC RESOURCE	HOW YOU ARE USING IT FOR HIS PURPOSES	STEPS TO USE THIS RESOURCE FOR HIS PURPOSES MORE
Work			
Abilities			
Gifts/Talents			

TYPE	SPECIFIC RESOURCE	HOW YOU ARE USING IT FOR HIS PURPOSES	STEPS TO USE THIS RESOURCE FOR HIS PURPOSES MORE
Education			
Finances			

Think of the last three times God called you step out and get started on a new undertaking. List each below and indicate if your initial response was to see it as an invitation or interruption.

#1: Step Called to Take:

Response:

#2: Step Called to Take:

_____

Response:

_____

#3: Step Called to Take:

_____

Response:

_____

What, if anything, do you want to change about your responses going forward and what can you do to make those changes?

9. Read these accounts of God doing a lot with a little. Take notes on what stands out to you about each one.

Exodus 4:1–9:

_____

Joshua 2:1–21:

_____

1 Samuel 17:1–51:

_____

2 Kings 4:1–7:

Mark 6:30–52:

In chapter 6 of *Don't Look Back*, "Go With What You Have," I write the following reminder:

> Whether we are working with a little or a lot, it never matters to God. What we think limits us doesn't limit him ... If each one of us will do what we can with what we have, even when it's just a little, our little will do a lot, not because of us, but because of God. Because of our obedience to God. Because of his faithfulness to us. Because of his willingness to help us with whatever he's put in our hearts to do. Sometimes, when we're stuck in a place, understanding this and then acting on it is what helps us move forward.

Write a prayer on the lines below asking God to remove any limits you've created for your life and that God would make your little into a whole lot.

IT'S TIME TO RISE UP

Our spiritual posture is one more thing that affects whether we are living our lives stuck looking back or intentionally moving forward with all the plans and purposes God has for us. If we're slouching, then by definition, we're drooped over; we're moving slowly or reluctantly; we're excessively relaxing our muscles to the point we're assuming an ungainly stooping of the head and shoulders. You could say we're looking down instead of up, that we've grown passive and laid back when God wants us on the edge of what he's doing and moving forward with him. Could it be that Lot's wife was slouching in some way? She certainly wasn't running for the hills with gusto because she stopped and looked back—and then she got stuck looking back for eternity. And none of us want that.

—**Christine Caine**, from Chapter 8 of *Don't Look Back*

Opening Discussion

Take five minutes and answer these questions to open your time before jumping into the video session.

1. On a scale of one to ten, how challenging is it for you to practice good physical posture?

   1 2 3 4 5 6 7 8 9 10

   I tend to bend over   I always sit up straight
   or slouch.   and practice good posture.

2. How would you describe your spiritual posture right now toward God and his plans and purposes for your life?

Session Five Video (22 minutes)

Group leader, stream the video or play the DVD.

As you watch, take notes on anything that stands out to you.

◆ Your posture matters

◆ Four men with leprosy

◆ Desperation can be a great gift

◆ Many of our gates are internal ones

_____

_____

_____

_____

_____

◆ What they thought was their end point was actually their access
  point

_____

_____

_____

_____

_____

◆ They became the voice of freedom to an entire city

_____

_____

_____

_____

_____

Group Discussion Questions

Group leader, read quotes and commentary aloud and use prompts to guide your discussion time.

> "I've found that we tend to suffer spiritually over time without even realizing it. Typically, our slouching goes unnoticed by us because we become comfortable in it, and we become really accustomed to it which means that, unless we're paying careful attention to our posture or unless someone brings it to our attention, we tend to overlook it." —Christine

1. In what areas of your spiritual life do you sense you're slouching in your relationship with God?

   Where do you most need to sit up, shoulders back, head tilted high in your response and obedience to God?

2. Select a volunteer to read **2 Kings 7:3–4**. Discuss the following questions regarding the passages:

   What drove the four men with leprosy to take action?

   Describe a time when you were in a similar "nothing to lose" situation. What happened and what was the result?

How have you experienced desperation as a gift to compel you to move forward?

3. Gates can become sources of security, familiarity, and comfort. Like the men with leprosy, where are you stuck at a gate that's already served its purpose?

Which of the following—security, familiarity, or comfort—is keeping you stuck in a place or position where God is calling you to move from?

What do you think God will do if you give up your security, familiarity, or comfort and move forward in obedience?

4. Select a few participants to split reading **2 Kings 7:5–11**. Discuss the following:

Describe the result of the daring men with leprosy leaving the familiarity of the gate. How was God on the move before the men with leprosy acted?

What would the men with leprosy have missed out on if they stayed stuck at the gate?

Describe a time when you moved forward and experienced God's provision and power. How would your life be different if you'd remained where you were?

"The men with leprosy, once sitting and starving, became the voice of freedom to an entire city. Why? Because they dared to change their posture, to change their perspective, to go from passively sitting to actively standing and moving forward. Because of that, they motivated an entire city to action and brought an end to everyone's starvation. That's one of the great things about freedom: Once we've tasted it, we want to go back to where we suffered and help everyone else taste it too. We want everyone to experience the same hope and provision." —Christine

5. How does doing daring things in obedience to God bless other people?

What's something good or beautiful or true that you've experienced in Christ that you can't keep to yourself?

6. Discuss the following:

What is the biggest takeaway for you from *Don't Look Back*?

What's one practical application from the study that you've put into practice?

What's one practical application from the study that you'd still like to do?

What changes have you noticed in your attitudes, actions, and behaviors as a result of this study?

Where are you expectant to see God move powerfully in your life?

Call to Action

Team up with someone in your group (or online if you are doing this study virtually) and share how this study has challenged and changed your spiritual posture. Pray for each other to become unstuck and that God gives you the strength and discipline to continue growing.

Conclusion

Group leader, read aloud to the group to close your time together this week.

Too often we frame things as though we are waiting for God, but what if God is waiting for us? What if God is calling us to let go of the familiar and comfortable, and take a risk? When we get unstuck, we often discover God is already on the move in the place we're going. Your greatest days are ahead of you and not behind you. Don't stop, don't get stuck, keep moving forward, and don't look back.

Closing Prayer

Select a volunteer to read the closing prayer over the group.

Jesus, our world has changed, and continues to change, but you have not changed. Your promises have not changed. Your plans for us have not changed. Your purpose for us has not changed. More than ever, it's time for us to rise up and move forward in bold faith. Give us the daring courage to take a risk, to stop looking back, to get unstuck, and to start moving forward into the fullness of your plans and purposes. Help us pursue you with everything we've got all the days of our lives. In your name we pray, amen.

Between Sessions Personal Study

This section is created as a guide for your personal study time to further explore the topics you discussed with your group as well as what you've learned from this study. If you're following along with my book, *Don't Look Back*, for the fullest experience of this message, read or review chapter 8

1. When have you faced a significant challenge or obstacle?

2. How, specifically, did you rise up on the inside before you rose up on the outside?

3. As you've grown in your relationship with God, what, if anything, would you do differently today to rise up inside if you faced that type of challenge again?

_____

_____

_____

_____

4. Reflect on your relationship with God over the years. Identify three to five times that you had a strong spiritual posture.

AGE	INDICATORS OF A SPIRITUALLY STRONG POSTURE

AGE	INDICATORS OF A SPIRITUALLY STRONG POSTURE

5. Now identify three to five times that you had a slouching spiritual posture.

AGE	INDICATORS OF A SPIRITUALLY SLOUCHING POSTURE

AGE	INDICATORS OF A SPIRITUALLY SLOUCHING POSTURE

Place the times you identified in the previous two charts in the chart on the next page. As you do, list them in chronological order, from youngest (top row) to oldest (bottom row).

Next, indicate whether the times were times of a spiritually strong posture by placing an X in that column or a spiritually slouching posture by placing an X in that column.

Now, identify any significant life circumstances at that age as well as the spiritual practices that you were committed to at that time.

6. Complete the chart.

AGE	SPIRITUALLY STRONG POSTURE	SPIRITUALLY SLOUCHING POSTURE	SIGNIFICANT LIFE CIRCUM-STANCES	SPIRITUAL PRACTICES

7. As you reflect on this chart, look at the times that you had a spiritually strong posture.

   What patterns or similarities do you notice about those periods— either in terms of life circumstances or spiritual practices?

   _____

   _____

   _____

   _____

   _____

8. Likewise, look at the times that you had a spiritually slouching posture. What patterns or similarities do you notice about those periods—either in terms of life circumstances or spiritual practices?

   _____

   _____

   _____

   _____

   _____

God has better for us than vacillating between spiritual strength/vitality and spiritual sluggishness/slouching. His desire is for us to be alive in him and available to be used by him for his purposes!

As you reflect on the questions you just worked through, take some time to pray:

God, I want to run the race of this life alive in you, filled with your strength, accomplishing your purposes for your praise. God, would you please open my eyes to learn from this exercise? What do I need to do today, and in the days ahead, to avoid spiritual apathy and slouching? And what do I need to do today, and in the days ahead, to grow in spiritual vitality and strength? What do I need to be on guard against? What practices do I need to put in place? What do I need to do differently? In Jesus' name, amen.

9. Write what comes to mind in the space below.

"Standing down is way easier than standing up, especially when we've been beaten down, knocked down, ridiculed, canceled, maligned, misunderstood, abandoned, or rejected; when everything seems hopeless, and we seem helpless. We must intentionally and frequently check our spiritual posture. If we're going to make it in the turbulent days in which we live, we're going to have to choose to look up and fix our eyes on Jesus, the pioneer and the perfecter of our faith. We are going to have to choose to rise up no matter how many times we fall down." —Christine

In chapter 8 of *Don't Look Back*, "Arise and Go: Things Change When We Do," I write the following reminder:

Because Jesus arose, we can arise. Because of Jesus, we can be the most hope-filled, faith-filled, joy-filled people on the planet. We can have more clarity, purpose, determination, strength, and endurance than anyone. We can be full of wisdom, creativity, vision, ideas, and projects. ... More than ever, it is time for us to arise. It's time for us to move on in bold faith, but that doesn't happen automatically. We have to rise up and do something with what we have right where we are, and we have to do it over and over each and every day.

Write a prayer on the lines below asking God to help you rise to new heights in him, his ways, his purposes, and his plans.

MEET CHRISTINE CAINE

Christine Caine is a speaker, activist, and bestselling author. She and her husband, Nick, founded the A21 Campaign, an anti–human trafficking organization. They also founded Propel Women, an initiative that is dedicated to coming alongside women all over the globe to activate their God-given purpose. You can tune into Christine's weekly podcast, *Equip & Empower*, or her TBN television program to be encouraged with the hope of Jesus wherever you are. To learn more about Christine, visit www.christinecaine.com.

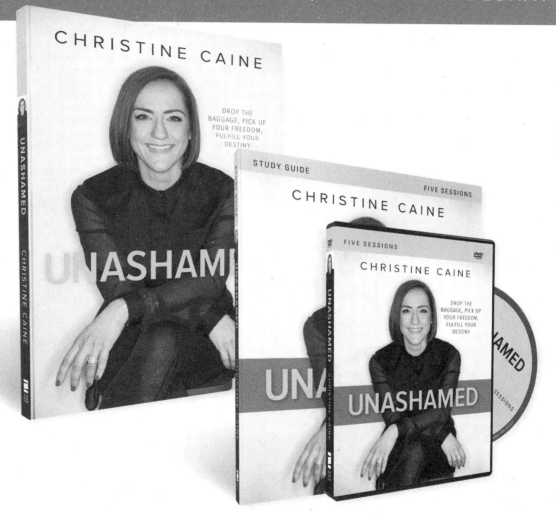

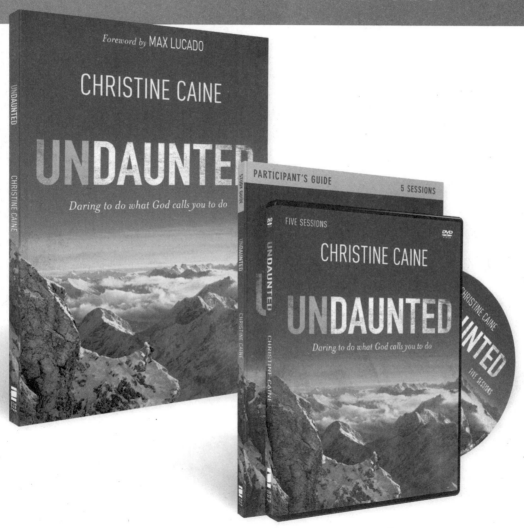

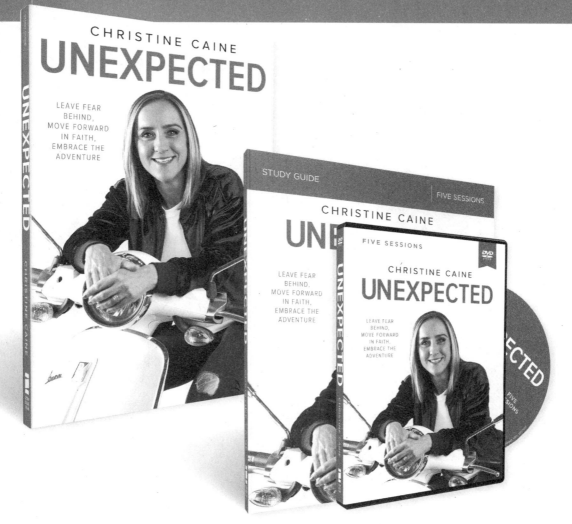

We hope you enjoyed this Bible study from **Christine Caine**. Here are some other Bible studies we think you'll like.

Jennie Allen

Get Out Of Your Head
VIDEO STUDY

Forgiving What You Can't Forget
VIDEO STUDY

Lysa TerKeurst

Our Mission
Equipping people to understand the Scriptures, cultivate spiritual growth, and live an inspired faith with Bible study and video resources from today's most trusted voices.

Megan Fate Marshman

Meant For Good
VIDEO STUDY

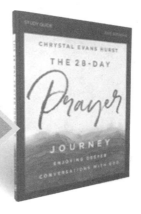

Chrystal Evans Hurst

The 28-Day Prayer Journal
VIDEO STUDY

Find your next Bible study, video series, or ministry training at:
HarperChristianResources.com

H HarperChristian Resources

Discover
new studies
from teachers you love, and

new teachers
we know you'll love!

Explore all these teachers and more.

Kasey Van Norman

Chrystal Evans Hurst

Jada Edwards

Wendy Speake

Christine Caine

Ann Voskamp

Ruth Chou Simons

Bianca Olthoff

Shannon Bream

Dr. Anita Phillips

Lisa Whittle

Karen Ehman

Hosanna Wong

Micah Maddox

Lysa TerKeurst

Rebekah Lyons

Sadie Robertson Huff

Wendy Blight

Madi Prewett Troutt

Anne Graham Lotz

Megan Marshman

Jennie Allen

Lynn Cowell

Lisa Harper

Allison Allen

Margaret Feinberg

Sarah Jakes Roberts

From the Publisher

GREAT STUDIES

ARE EVEN BETTER WHEN THEY'RE SHARED!

Help others find this study:

- Post a review at your favorite online bookseller.

- Post a picture on a social media account and share why you enjoyed it.

- Send a note to a friend who would also love it or, better yet, go through it with them.

Thanks for helping others grow their faith!